1 John, 2 John, 3 John & Jude: a Verse by Verse Bible Study

Non Pauline and General Epistles, Volume 2

Dr Andrew C S Koh

Published by Dr. Andrew C S Koh, 2022.

Copyright

Scan QR code for a free audiobook

Table of Contents

Dedicated to my wife, my sons, my daughters-in-law, my grandsons, my granddaughters, and to the glory of God

Foreword

Archbishop Ng Moon Hing

Anglican Archbishop of Southeast Asia

Both the apostle John and Jude lived in the period where the persecution of Christians was on the rise in the Roman Empire. While both great men were instructing and helping fellow Christians to hold on to their faithfulness, in their belief of Jesus Christ as their Savior and Lord, they were also teaching them to discern the false prophets and heretics who came to devour the Christians from within their churches from the true ones.

The authors of these four epistles have indeed led their readers to appreciate and focus on the specific teachings of the apostle John and Jude; that is, salvation has a price—it engages with the whole person. One of the main issues that has weakened the Christian Church is sin, which includes sin in the head, body, heart and limbs. To overcome sin from the *head*, we must believe in Jesus Christ, who can forgive sins (1 John 5:10); from the *body*, it is the love of our brethren that creates unity and fellowship in the Lord (1 John 4:12, 19); from the *heart*, it is the faithfulness that obeys the commandments of the Lord (1 John 3:21–24); from the *limbs*, it is the walking of the second mile to find and encourage those who are lost to trust in Christ Jesus (Jude 22–23). This sin was, and is, caused by false teachers who are under the influence of the evil ones, causing big headaches for the church then and now. The way forward is to identify these heretics and reject their teachings, even if they seem innocent, and draw lines to demarcate their influence. A total dependence on the Lord Jesus Christ, under the guidance of the Holy Spirit and according to the grace of God the Father, will be able to steer us out of the dominance of false teachers. Glory to God in the highest.

I thank the author for highlighting the truth so clearly in his verse-by-verse exposition. This is a great work and an excellent effort to assist Christians, especially new believers, in understanding of the Word of truth.

Testimonials

Rev. Ng Wah Lok (former Principal of Tung Ling Seminary Malaysia, 1999–2019)

"1, 2, 3 John, and Jude are books rarely studied by Christians. 1, 2, 3 John are very late writings of the apostle John and contain important teachings to counter false teachers and early Gnosticism. They are very applicable to our modern church because there are many false teachers and prophets who preach corrupt doctrines today.

"Andrew Koh has given a clear background and simple explanations of every passage in 1, 2, 3 John, and Jude. At the end of each chapter, he gives a devotional application and prayer. There are 11 lessons so you can use this study guide as 11 Bible Studies over 11 weeks. Any student who goes through this study guide carefully will gain a good foundational understanding of 1, 2, 3 John and Jude.

"Great work! This helps Christians, especially new and young believers, understand the Word of Truth."

Kevin Booker

"I found the book to be a great study guide and a great time to reflect on myself. I recommend this book to anyone who wants to understand faith in the Books of 1, 2, 3 John and Jude better."

Tiffany Townsend

"This book contains an explanation of the books of 1, 2, 3 John, as well as Jude. The books are formatted in an easy-to-follow and enjoyable way."

J. Sharmani

"This was a wonderful instruction in the Books of 1, 2, 3 John and Jude. Dr. Koh's simple lessons in these books of the Bible are so enlightening."

PAR

"To learn and apply the teachings of Jesus Christ, start by studying and understanding the books of 1, 2, 3 John and Jude. This devotional is a verse-by-verse expositional commentary on 1, 2, 3 John and Jude. It is taught as a Christ-centered, life-changing commentary, both a Bible study guide and a devotional guide."

Preface

1 John, 2 John, 3 John, and Jude is an in-depth Bible study that offers readers the opportunity to explore the Word of God and encounter its God. Written by Dr. Andrew C. S. Koh, this devotional and teaching aid is a comprehensive guide to the Scriptures, providing daily lessons with opening prayer, exposition, application, and closing prayer. Each lesson provides a unique perspective on the text, emphasizing its place in our faith and exploring its relevance to daily life.

This book is perfect for believers looking to deepen their understanding of Scripture. It is an ideal companion for individuals who want to grow in their faith by reflecting on a particular passage of the Bible. For those who are seeking a deeper spiritual experience, *1 John, 2 John, 3 John, and Jude* is an invaluable source of knowledge and insight.

Featuring study questions, personal reflections, and an engaging examination of the Word of God, this book provides a comprehensive guide to uncovering the divine message. Comparable to popular works such as *Bible Study for Beginners* by R. T. Kendall and *The Jesus Bible Study* by Jack Kuhatschek, *1 John, 2 John, 3 John, and Jude* is an accessible and informative source for those wanting to understand the Bible better.

For readers looking to experience a deeper connection with the Word of God, *1 John, 2 John, 3 John, and Jude* is an essential guide. Through this verse-by-verse Bible study, readers can open their hearts and minds to the power of the Scriptures and find a true spiritual connection. Read this book and discover the God of the Word today.

Dr. Andrew C. S. Koh

June 2021

1

Introduction to 1 John

Prayer

Heavenly Father, we pray for wisdom to tap into Your knowledge through daily devotion, daily reading of Your Word, and daily Bible study. We pray for wisdom, knowledge, and understanding of Scripture. In Jesus' name, amen.

Authorship

Scholars agree that the apostle John, who wrote the Gospel of John and Revelation, was the author of 1, 2, and 3 John. They are believed to have been written in Ephesus between AD 85 and 95. John was the last remaining apostle of Christ and was a very old man when he wrote 1, 2, and 3 John.

Audience

1 John is a general epistle and a cyclical letter written to a group of churches in the region around the city of Ephesus, in the west of modern-day Turkey.

Occasion and Purpose

John wrote 1 John to address the false teachers who came to deceive the Christians with the heretical teachings of Gnosticism. *Gnosis* is Greek for knowledge. These teachers claimed that they had special knowledge about salvation that others did not have.

The Gnostics believed that the soul is intrinsically good and the body is intrinsically evil. The Gnostics accepted the deity of Christ but rejected his humanity. They believed that Jesus was hundred percent divine but zero percent human. They believed that when He walked on the earth, He did not leave any footprint behind Him.

There are two extreme forms of Gnosticism. The one is asceticism, the denial of all the physical pleasures of life. The other extreme is licentiousness and freedom to sin, since the body is intrinsically evil and

"

headed for destruction anyway. John's purpose was to refute the heretical teachings of the Gnostics and to bring the people back to correct theology.

1 John 1:1–4, John declared what he saw, heard, and handled

Verse 1, *That which was from the beginning, that which we have heard, that which we have seen with our eyes, that which we saw, and our hands touched, concerning the Word of life.*

Reflection

The beginning alludes to Genesis 1:1, *in the beginning, God created the heavens and the earth*, and John 1:1, *in the beginning was the Word, and the Word was with God, and the Word was God*. John's title for Jesus Christ is Word of life, He who pre-existed creation, time, and space. John proclaimed that Christ is both fully God and fully human. He could be seen, heard and touched. In the Gospel of John, Christ could feel thirsty, hungry, tired, be sad, and weep.

Verses 2–4, 2 *(and the life was revealed, and we have seen, and testify, and declare to you the life, the eternal life, which was with the Father, and was revealed to us); 3 that which we have seen and heard we declare to you, that you also may have fellowship with us. Yes, and our fellowship is with the Father, and with his Son, Jesus Christ. 4 And we write these things to you, that our joy may be fulfilled.*

Reflection

Greek for life is *zoe*, which means God-given divine or eternal life. Greek for manifest is *phaneroo*, which means to make visible. Jesus, the word of eternal life, was made visible through His incarnation. John and the other apostles witnessed, declared, handled, heard, and fellowshipped with the incarnate word of life. God invites us into fellowship with Him and His Son Jesus Christ so that our joy may be complete.

Application

Testify about the eternal life that Jesus offers. Find opportunities to tell your story of how Jesus changed your life. You can do this by sharing your testimony on social media or in conversations with family and friends. By sharing Jesus with others, they can see the life and hope He offers.

Participate actively in your faith community. Engage more deeply in your church or small groups. To strengthen your faith, you can attend meetings, participate in group activities, and connect with other believers. True fellowship encourages you to live the gospel together and strengthens your faith.

Enjoy your relationship with Jesus, and with your fellow believers. Nurture your spiritual life and build relationships with other Christians. Prioritize time spent with God, in scripture and prayer. Furthermore, foster significant relationships with fellow believers. You can then experience the joy of living in God's love and truth.

Jesus Christ is the pre-existing, self-existing, eternal Son of God. He is co-equal, co-divine, and co-eternal with the Father, sharing the same Godhead. John testified that Jesus Christ is fully divine and fully man and refuted the Gnostic claim that Jesus is divine but not human.

Prayer

Heavenly Father, we claim the promise of Isaiah 55:11, that Your Word will not return to You empty but will accomplish what You desire and achieve the purpose for which You sent it. We pray for wisdom to understand, apply, and obey Your teachings. In Jesus' name, amen.

2

Walk in the Light of Christ

Prayer

Heavenly Father, we acknowledge that Your Son, Jesus, is the bright morning star, the lily of the valley, rose of Sharon, ancient of days, kinsmen redeemer, Holy One of God, Holy One of Israel, and Holy One of Jacob. We pray for open, receptive, soft, obedient, and teachable spirits. In Jesus' name, amen.

1 John 1:5–10

Verse 5,*This is the message which we have heard from him and announce to you, that God is light, and in him is no darkness at all.*

Reflection

Jesus is the word of God. Greek for word is *logos*, which means message. John declared to his readers, and us, that he and the apostles had heard the message of God from Jesus. Jesus is the light of life, who shines His light into the dark world. Jesus is light and whoever walks with Him will not stumble in darkness.

1 John 1:1, *That which was from the beginning, which we have heard, which we have seen with our eyes, which we have looked upon, and our hands have handled, concerning the Word of life.*

John 1:4, *In Him was life, and the life was the light of men.*

John 8:12, *Then Jesus spoke to them again, saying, "I am the light of the world. He who follows Me shall not walk in darkness, but have the light of life."*

John 9:5, *As long as I am in the world, I am the light of the world.*

Verse 6, *If we say that we have fellowship with him and walk in the darkness, we lie, and don't tell the truth.*

Reflection

We cannot have fellowship with Jesus if we continue to live in sin or walk in darkness, deception, and falsehood. The light of Jesus removes darkness, exposing lies. We cannot hide anything before Jesus, because He is the all-knowing omniscient God.

Hebrews 4:13, *And there is no creature hidden from His sight, but all things are naked and open to the eyes of Him to whom we must give account.*

Verse 7, *But if we walk in the light, as he is in the light, we have fellowship with one another, and the blood of Jesus Christ, his Son, cleanses us from all sin*

Reflection

If we walk in the light of Christ and are cleansed of sins, we can have fellowship with Him and with our fellow Christians.

Verses 8–10, *8 If we say that we have no sin, we deceive ourselves, and the truth is not in us. 9 If we confess our sins, he is faithful and righteous to forgive us the sins, and to cleanse us from all unrighteousness. 10 If we say that we haven't sinned, we make him a liar, and his word is not in us.*

Reflection

No one can claim to be sinless, for all have sinned and fallen short of God's perfect standard, Romans 3:23. If we sin, we should come before Jesus, confess and repent of our sin. Jesus is faithful and will forgive our sin and purify us, 1 John 1:9. If we insist that we are sinless, we are not living in the truth of God's words.

Romans 3:23, *for all have sinned and fall short of the glory of God.*

1 John 1:9, *If we confess our sins, He is faithful and just to forgive us our sins and to cleanse us from all unrighteousness.*

Application

Walking in God's light means making decisions that reflect his truth and holiness. For example, being honest, maintaining your integrity, showing kindness and avoiding actions that lead to darkness. This strengthens your relationship with Him and others.

Openness and action can create a genuine community. Be honest in your interactions with other Christians. This will foster a trusting environment that encourages accountability, sharing of struggles and encouragement.

Truthfulness is important, both to yourself and God. Regularly examine your actions before God and confess any sins you may have committed. This will help you to be more humble, stay on track with His will and allow you to receive His forgiveness and grace. Confession is essential to maintaining a close and trusting relationship between you and the Almighty.

To accept God's mercy and move forward with righteousness, you must not only receive forgiveness, but also recommit yourself to living a righteous life. It is through accepting His mercy that you are freed from the weight of guilt, and can experience spiritual growth.

Don't minimize or dismiss your sins. To be honest with God and yourself, admit any weaknesses or sins you may have, such as pride or self-deception. This requires that you are vigilant in avoiding prideful self-deception and seeking the truth daily from Him. Integrity and spiritual growth are dependent on being honest with yourself and God.

Walk in the truth of Holy Spirit. Be transparent before Him. But if you sin, you should confess your sin before Him and repent. Claim the promise of 1 John 1:9 for the forgiveness of sin and cleansing.

Prayer

Heavenly Father, we praise You and thank You because You are worthy to be praised. You are the name above all names, You are light and there is no darkness in You. We pray that You will help us to walk in the light of Christ. In Jesus' name, amen.

3

The Tests of Knowing Christ

Prayer

Heavenly Father, we acknowledge that Your Son Jesus is Emmanuel, Lamb of God, Lion of Judah, Shepherd and Captain of our souls. We pray for soft, faithful, obedient, teachable, and sensitive spirits to tap into Your goodness, grace, and love. In Jesus' name, amen.

1 John 2:1–11

Verses 1–2, *1 My little children, I write these things to you so that you may not sin. If anyone sins, we have a Counselor with the Father, Jesus Christ, the righteous. 2 And he is the atoning sacrifice for our sins, and not for ours only, but also for the whole world.*

Reflection

John, the last surviving apostle of Christ, addressed his audience tenderly as little children. As Christians, we are not to habitually sin, but if we sin, we have Jesus Christ as our Advocate with the Father. Greek for advocate is *parakletos*, which means counselor or defense attorney. Greek for propitiation is *hilasterion*, which means the mercy seat. The mercy seat was the golden cover on the ark of the covenant, which was kept in the Holy of Holies.

Before the destruction of the temple, the high priest entered the Holy of Holies once a year on Yom Kippur, the Day of Atonement, to sacrifice a lamb and splash the blood of the lamb onto the mercy seat as atonement for the sins of the Israelites for one year. On Good Friday, Jesus Christ died on the cross as a substitutionary atonement for our sins. He meets us on the mercy seat of the "ark of the covenant" to forgive our sins.

Verses 3–6, *3 This is how we know that we know him: if we keep his commandments. 4 One who says, "I know him," and doesn't keep his commandments, is a liar, and the truth isn't in him. 5 But God's love has most certainly been perfected in whoever keeps his word. This is how we know that we are in him: 6 he who says he remains in him ought himself also to walk just like he walked.*

Reflection

The tests of knowing Christ are obedience to His commands, love for God, and love for people. We cannot claim to know Christ if we do not obey His commands. Christ is truth. The test of knowing Him is to walk in truth. Christ is love. Another test of knowing Christ is to walk in love, vertical love for God, and horizontal love for people. Greek for abide is *meno*, which means remain or endure. If we remain in Him, we will obey Him and conduct our lives according to His commandments.

Verses 7–8, *7 Brothers, I write no new commandment to you, but an old commandment which you had from the beginning. The old commandment is the word which you heard from the beginning. 8 Again, I write a new commandment to you, which is true in him and in you; because the darkness is passing away and the true light already shines.*

Reflection

The old commandment is from the Old Testament: to love the Lord with all your heart, with all your soul, and with all your strength. The new commandment is from the New Testament: to love another as Christ loved us. The true light of Christ's righteousness had come to remove the darkness of evil in the world.

Deuteronomy 6:5, *You shall love the Lord your God with all your heart, with all your soul, and with all your strength.*

John 13:34, *A new commandment I give to you, that you love one another; as I have loved you, that you also love one another.*

John 1:5, *And the light shines in the darkness, and the darkness did not comprehend it.*

Verses 9–11, *9 He who says he is in the light and hates his brother is in the darkness even until now. 10 He who loves his brother remains in the light, and there is no occasion for stumbling in him. 11 But he who hates his brother is in the darkness, and walks in the darkness, and doesn't know where he is going, because the darkness has blinded his eyes.*

Reflection

Christ is light. Another test of knowing Christ is to walk in His light. We are to walk in the light of Christ and love our brother. If we hate our brother, we are in darkness and deception and the light of Christ is not in us. Light is symbolic of Christ, truth, righteousness, and goodness. Darkness is symbolic of Satan, deception, sin, and evil.

Application

Take a moment to consider how you deal with guilt and sin. Instead of feeling guilty when you sin and being ashamed, let Jesus be your advocate to the Father.

Think about how you live out your faith and obey God's commands. Follow Jesus' teachings, love mercy, act justly, and walk humbly before Him every day.

Think about how you treat others. In all your relationships, emulate Christ's love by demonstrating genuine, selfless caring for others. This could include actively seeking out opportunities to encourage and support each other.

Reflect on your interactions with other people. Show mercy and love to everyone, acting as if you are the light of Christ. Directly address any conflict or negative feelings to create peace in relationships.

Consider any areas that are dark in your heart. Instead of hating or feeling bitter, seek help from God to replace negative emotions with his light and love. You can heal yourself and others by praying, forgiving others and changing your attitude and behavior.

Do not to sin habitually; but if you sin, come before Jesus Christ in confession and repentance. If we confess your sins, He is faithful and just and will forgive and cleanse you of all your unrighteousness. Walk in obedience, in truth, in love, in the light, in the Holy Spirit, and in Christ. These are the tests of knowing Christ.

Prayer

Heavenly Father, we confess that we are sinners saved by grace. We pray for forgiveness of sin, justification, salvation, sanctification, and eternal life. We pray for divine guidance and enablement to walk in obedience, in Christ, in the Holy Spirit, in truth, in light, and in faith. In Jesus' name, amen.

4

Do Not Love the World

Prayer

Heavenly Father, we come before You again to study Your Word. We pray that You will speak to us through the pages of Scripture. We pray for enlightenment by the Holy Spirit. We pray for eyes to see and ears to hear. In Jesus' name, amen.

1 John 2:12–29

Verses 12–14, *12 I write to you, little children, because your sins are forgiven you for his name's sake. 13 I write to you, fathers, because you know him who is from the beginning. I write to you, young men, because you have overcome the evil one. I write to you, little children, because you know the Father. 14 I have written to you, fathers, because you know him who is from the beginning. I have written to you, young men, because you are strong, and the word of God remains in you, and you have overcome the evil one.*

Reflection

John wrote to three categories of people: little children in the faith, new believers; fathers in the faith, mature believers; and young men in the faith, those in between the two extremes. John commended them because their sins were forgiven, they knew Christ, they had overcome Satan, they were strong in the faith, and they knew the Word of God.

Verses 15–17, *15 Don't love the world or the things that are in the world. If anyone loves the world, the Father's love isn't in him. 16 For all that is in the world, the lust of the flesh, the lust of the eyes, and the pride of life, isn't the Father's, but is the world's. 17 The world is passing away with its lusts, but he who does God's will remains forever.*

Reflection

Greek for "love" in all of 1 John is *agape*, which means the divine love of God for people. Greek for "world" is *kosmos*, which means the earth. We should not love or be too attached to the things of this world.

16

Although we live on earth, our real citizenship is heaven. Greek for pass away is *parago*, which means disappear. This world will disappear soon, as Jesus' second coming is imminent. The lust of the flesh speaks of the desires of the flesh. The lust of the eyes speaks of covetousness. The pride of life speaks of arrogance.

Satan tempted Jesus with these in the desert and on the mount of temptation, but Jesus overcame him by the Word of God. Satan tempted Jesus to satisfy his hunger by changing stones to bread (the lust of the flesh), showed Him the kingdoms of the world (lust of the eyes), and tempted Him to defy God by jumping off the pinnacle of the temple (pride of life).

Eve was also tempted by Satan in these three areas, and he deceived her. The fruit that looked good for food speaks of the lust of the flesh. The fruit was pleasant to the eyes, which speaks of the lust of the eyes. The tree was also desirable to make one wise, which speaks of the pride of life.

Genesis 3:6, *So when the woman saw that the tree was good for food, that it was pleasant to the eyes, and a tree desirable to make one wise, she took of its fruit and ate.*

Verse *18, Little children, these are the end times, and as you heard that the Antichrist is coming, even now many antichrists have arisen. By this we know that it is the final hour.*

Reflection

John warned his audience, and us, about the imminent second coming of Christ and the arrival of the Antichrist on the world scene. The Antichrist will be a ruthless dictator who will rule the earth during the last 3.5 years of world history called the great tribulation. He is also called the beast, the man of lawlessness, and the son of perdition.

Verses 19–23, *19 They went out from us, but they didn't belong to us; for if they had belonged to us, they would have continued with us. But they left, that they might be revealed that none of them belong to us. 20 You have an anointing from the Holy One, and you all have knowledge. 21 I have not written to you because you don't know the truth, but because you know it, and because no lie is of the truth. 22 Who is the liar but he who denies that Jesus is the Christ? This is the Antichrist, he who denies the Father and the Son. 23 Whoever denies the Son doesn't have the Father. He who confesses the Son has the Father also.*

Reflection

They who *went out from us, but were not of us* speaks of the heretical gnostic teachers. The anointing of the Holy Spirit should enable Christians to discern truth from lies. Anyone who denies Jesus as the Christ and the Father as God is an antichrist. Whoever denies Christ, denies the Father. Whoever acknowledges Christ, acknowledges the Father.

Verse 24, *24 Therefore, as for you, let that remain in you which you heard from the beginning. If that which you heard from the beginning remains in you, you also will remain in the Son, and in the Father.*

Reflection

John encouraged his disciples, and us, to abide in Christ and in the Father.

Verses 25–27, *25 This is the promise which he promised us, the eternal life. 26 These things I have written to you concerning those who would lead you astray. 27 As for you, the anointing which you received from him remains in you, and you don't need for anyone to teach you. But as his anointing teaches you concerning all things, and is true, and is no lie, and even as it taught you, you will remain in him.*

Reflection

We have the promise of eternal life from Christ. John warned his audience, and us, not to be deceived by the false teachings of the Gnostics. If we abide in Christ, His anointing on us will teach us all things.

Verses 28–29, *28 Now, little children, remain in him, that when he appears, we may have boldness, and not be ashamed before him at his coming. 29 If you know that he is righteous, you know that everyone who practices righteousness has been born of him.*

Reflection

John encouraged his audience, and us, to abide in Christ so they would be confident and not ashamed at His second coming. Christ is righteous and those who practice righteousness are His children.

Application

Regularly reflecting upon and assessing one's spiritual journey and development is of utmost importance. Evaluate your progress and identify areas in which further growth could take place. Acknowledge God's forgiveness, knowledge, and strength that He has provided you. Celebrate triumphs over sin by simultaneously deepening your understanding and maturing spiritually through consistent contemplation of spiritual matters. Doing this keeps you encouraged and motivated for continued spiritual growth!

Reexamine your desires and priorities carefully, without giving into worldly temptations. Think about whether you are putting more importance on worldly desires than on loving God. Check how you are using your time, money, and energy to see if it is in line with His will. Avoiding worldly temptations helps keep focus on what truly matters while strengthening your relationship with the Lord.

Be mindful of your spiritual discernment. Be careful of false teachings that go against God's word. Read your Bible regularly and seek advice from trusted Christian mentors for guidance on matters related to your faith. Staying alert helps protect it while assuring that you follow the correct path.

Reflect upon how God is leading your life with the help of the Holy Spirit. Rely upon his anointing and truth. Try to connect with God through prayer, meditation, and obedience. Accepting His anointing can help you understand the truth and live according to His will.

Reevaluate your confession of faith. Acknowledging Jesus boldly as Christ will strengthen both your own faith and witness to others.

Reaffirming it may mean more openly sharing and defending it when necessary, and holding fast to this truth strengthens both.

Reevaluate how well you adhere to Christ's teachings. Apply what you've learned into daily life. Regularly study Scripture, follow its lessons, and let it shape your identity and actions. Staying aligned with God's promises is essential!

Consider your readiness for Christ's return. Focus on living righteously and with an expectation of His return. Try to be like Him in all you do, by being honest, kind, and fair in your daily life. Doing this keeps eternal priorities at the forefront and ensures you're ready when He arrives again!

You do not belong to the world. Do not to hold too tightly to the things of the world. You are not immortal and the world will not last forever. Your real citizenship is in heaven. One day, you will be with Christ in heaven until eternity. Your years of earthly existence are insignificant compared to eternity. Invest in the things of the Kingdom that will last into eternity.

Prayer

Heavenly Father, we confess that we sometimes sin. We pray for forgiveness of our sins and help to obey Your calling. Help us not to cling to the things of the world but to the things of Your kingdom. We pray for Your kingdom perspective. In Jesus' name, amen.

5

Behold What Manner of Love

Prayer

Heavenly Father, we pray for mercy, grace, wisdom, and understanding into the reading of Your Word. We pray You help us unlock the meaning of difficult and controversial verses. In Jesus' name, amen.

1 John 3:1–24

Verses 1–3, *1 See how great a love the Father has given to us, that we should be called children of God! For this cause the world doesn't know us, because it didn't know him. 2 Beloved, now we are children of God. It is not yet revealed what we will be; but we know that when he is revealed, we will be like him; for we will see him just as he is. 3 Everyone who has this hope set on him purifies himself, even as he is pure.*

Reflection

Greek for behold is *horao*, which means consider. John encouraged his audience, and us, to consider the magnitude of God's love for us when He adopted us into His family after we accepted Christ as our Lord and Saviour. The word love appears repeatedly in 1 John and as already mentioned, the Greek word for love is always *agape*.

Agape is the highest form of love, the divine sacrificial love of God for people. The world rejected us because it rejected God. When Christ comes back, at the rapture He will resurrect us into glorified bodies to meet Him in the clouds.

1 Thessalonians 4:17, *After that, we who are still alive and are left will be caught up together with them in the clouds to meet the Lord in the air. And so we will be with the Lord forever.*

Verses 4–6, *4 Everyone who sins also commits lawlessness. Sin is lawlessness. 5 You know that he was revealed to take away our sins, and no sin is in him. 6 Whoever remains in him doesn't sin. Whoever sins hasn't seen him and doesn't know him.*

Reflection

Greek for sin is *hamartia*, which means missing the mark. Greek for lawlessness is *anomia*, which means transgression. Whoever misses the mark of God's perfect standard has transgressed against God. The problem of sin had been dealt with on the cross. Christ paid the penalty of our sins on the cross of Calvary on Good Friday. Whoever walks in obedience to Christ will not walk in sin because Christ is sinless.

Verses 7–9, *7 Little children, let no one lead you astray. He who does righteousness is righteous, even as he is righteous. 8 He who sins is of the devil, for the devil has been sinning from the beginning. To this end the Son of God was revealed: that he might destroy the works of the devil. 9 Whoever is born of God doesn't commit sin, because his seed remains in him, and he can't sin, because he is born of God.*

Reflection

John warned his audience, and us, not to be deceived by the Gnostic teachers. Whoever practices righteousness is righteous just as Christ is righteous. Whoever practices wickedness is from Satan. Christ came to earth to destroy the works of Satan. Those who are spiritually regenerated will not habitually sin because they are born of God.

Verses 10–12, *10 In this the children of God are revealed, and the children of the devil. Whoever doesn't do righteousness is not of God, neither is he who doesn't love his brother. 11 For this is the message which you heard from the beginning, that we should love one another; 12 unlike Cain, who was of the evil one, and killed his brother. Why did he kill him? Because his deeds were evil, and his brother's righteous.*

Reflection

John compared the children of God, Christians, with the children of Satan, non-Christians. The children of God practice righteousness, whereas the children of Satan practice wickedness. The children of God practice love, whereas the children of Satan practice wickedness.

We are to love one another just as Christ loves us. John compared Cain, a son of Satan, with Abel, a son of God. God rejected Cain's unrighteous sacrifice but accepted Abel's righteous sacrifice. Cain murdered his brother because he was wicked and his brother was righteous.

Verses 13–15, *13 Don't be surprised, my brothers, if the world hates you. 14 We know that we have passed out of death into life, because we love the brothers. He who doesn't love his brother remains in death. 15 Whoever hates his brother is a murderer, and you know that no murderer has eternal life remaining in him.*

Reflection

John warned his audience, and us, not to be surprised if the world hates us because the world hates God. We are to love our brother and not to hate him. To hate our brother is to murder him in our heart. Jesus said in the beatitude that murder begins in the heart.

Matthew 5:21–22, *You have heard that it was said to those of old, "You shall not murder, and whoever murders will be in danger of the judgment." But I say to you that whoever is angry with his brother without a cause shall be in danger of the judgment. And whoever says to his brother, "Raca!" shall be in danger of the council.*

Verses 16–17, *16 By this we know love, because he laid down his life for us. And we ought to lay down our lives for the brothers. 17 But whoever has the world's goods and sees his brother in need, then closes his heart of compassion against him, how does God's love remain in him?*

Reflection

Christ demonstrated His love for us when He died on the cross for us while we were still sinners. We are to love our brothers in the same way that Christ loved us. We are to help our brother if he needs our help and if we are in a position to meet that need.

Romans 5:8, *But God demonstrates His own love toward us, in that while we were still sinners, Christ died for us.*

Verses 18–20, *18 My little children, let's not love in word only, or with the tongue only, but in deed and truth. 19 And by this we know that we are of the truth, and persuade our hearts before him, 20 because if our heart condemns us, God is greater than our heart, and knows all things.*

Reflection

John warned his audience, and us, not to love in words alone but in action and truth because we are of the truth. Greek for condemn is *kataginosko*, which means accuse. If our heart accuses us of sin, God is greater than our heart and will not accuse us of sin.

Romans 8:1, *There is therefore now no condemnation to them which are in Christ Jesus, who walk not after the flesh, but after the Spirit.*

Verses 21–23, *21 Beloved, if our hearts don't condemn us, we have boldness toward God; 22 so whatever we ask, we receive from him, because we keep his commandments and do the things that are pleasing in his sight. 23 This is his commandment, that we should believe in the name of his Son, Jesus Christ, and love one another, even as he commanded.*

Reflection

Greek for boldness is *parresia*, which means confidence to speak. If our heart does not accuse us, we can come before God with boldness in prayer and He will answer us. We are to believe in the name of Christ and love one another as Christ loved us.

Hebrews 4:16, *Let us, therefore, come boldly to the throne of grace, that we may obtain mercy and find grace to help in time of need.*

Ephesians 3:12, *in whom we have boldness and access with confidence through faith in Him.*

John 13:34, *A new commandment I give to you, that you love one another; as I have loved you, that you also love one another.*

Verse 24, *24 He who keeps his commandments remains in him, and he in him. By this we know that he remains in us, by the Spirit which he gave us.*

Reflection

John encouraged his audience, and us, to keep Christ's commandments and remain in Him. Christ will abide in us through the indwelling of the Holy Spirit.

John 15:4, *Abide in Me, and I in you. As the branch cannot bear fruit of itself, unless it abides in the vine, neither can you, unless you abide in Me.*

Application

Consider your identity as a child of Christ. Remind yourself every day of God's unconditional love for you and your status as his child. As a member of God's extended family, you should live with dignity and confidence.

Consider your pursuit of purity. Purify your life. Avoid sin, and strive for holiness in all your thoughts, words, and actions. It involves regular self-examination, and asking God for help in growing in righteousness.

Consider your attitude towards sin. Your approach to sin can have a profound impact on your personal growth and well-being. Take sin very seriously and work to overcome it. Adopt righteousness and reject sinful habits and behaviors. To do this, you must rely on God for strength and guidance every day to resist temptations and do the right thing.

Consider how you show love to others. Consider practical ways to show love, like helping others in need, being kind, and showing patience and understanding. True love is based on self-sacrifice, and the willingness to put other people's needs ahead of your own.

Consider any feelings of hatred and resentment that you may harbor. Forgive those who have hurt me and let go of bitterness. By overcoming hatred, you can allow God's love in your life and heart to flourish.

Consider your compassion and generosity. As much as possible, help those who are in need. Be more aware of the needs of other people and willing to give your time, resources and effort to help them. Compassionate acts are an expression of God's unconditional love.

Consider how you deal with guilt and self-condemnation. Trust in God's understanding and forgiveness. You can bring your doubts, guilt feelings and questions to God and trust in His forgiveness and greater knowledge. You can live in confidence and trust His grace, without being paralyzed or weighed down by the past.

Consider your obedience to God. Love others and believe in Jesus. Show your love for Jesus and your belief in him through all your actions to renew your commitment to faith. Your relationship with God, and those around you, is strengthened by living in obedience.

God loved you with an everlasting love. Christ's death on the cross showed the extent of His love. Love is one of the tests of knowing Christ. Love God vertically and love your brothers and sisters in Christ horizontally. Love is the greatest of the Ten Commandments and is the greatest virtue of all.

1 Corinthians 13:13, *And now abide faith, hope, love, these three, but the greatest of these is love.*

Jeremiah 31:3, *The Lord has appeared of old to me, saying: "Yes, I have loved you with an everlasting love; Therefore with lovingkindness, I have drawn you."*

Prayer

Heavenly Father, thank You for sending Jesus Christ to be our Lord and Saviour. Thank You for Your love, mercy, and grace. We pray for the grace to love You, to love our brothers and sisters in Christ and our neighbors. We pray for divine enablement to keep Your commandments and abide in Your love. In Jesus' name, amen.

6

God Is Love

Prayer

Heavenly Father, thank You for allowing us to meet You again in daily devotion. We pray for a relationship, fellowship, and communication with You. We pray that You speak to us as only You can. In Jesus' name, amen.

1 John 4:1–11

Verses 1–3, *1 Beloved, don't believe every spirit, but test the spirits, whether they are of God, because many false prophets have gone out into the world. 2 By this you know the Spirit of God: every spirit who confesses that Jesus Christ has come in the flesh is of God, 3 and every spirit who doesn't confess that Jesus Christ has come in the flesh is not of God, and this is the spirit of the Antichrist, of whom you have heard that it comes. Now it is in the world already.*

Reflection

John warned his audience, and us, to test and discern every spirit because not all spirits are from God. Some spirits are from false prophets who belong to Satan. Every spirit that acknowledges the incarnation of Christ is from God. Every spirit that denies the incarnation of Christ is the spirit of the Antichrist. John refuted the Gnostic teachers, who denied the incarnation of Christ.

Verses 4–6, *4 You are of God, little children, and have overcome them; because greater is he who is in you than he who is in the world. 5 They are of the world. Therefore they speak of the world, and the world hears them. 6 We are of God. He who knows God listens to us. He who is not of God doesn't listen to us. By this we know the spirit of truth, and the spirit of error.*

Reflection

1 John 4:4 is a beautiful memory verse, *He who is in you is greater than he who is in the world.* The Holy Spirit who is in us is greater than

Satan, who is in the world. The world listens to non-Christians, who belong to it. God listens to Christians, who belong to Him, but will not listen to non-Christians, who do not belong to Him.

Verses 7–9, *7 Beloved, let's love one another, for love is of God; and everyone who loves has been born of God, and knows God. 8 He who doesn't love doesn't know God, for God is love. 9 By this God's love was revealed in us, that God has sent his one and only Son into the world that we might live through him.*

Reflection

John encouraged his audience, and us, to love one another because God is love. To know God is to love Him. We are to love God vertically and love one another horizontally. God sent His Son into the world because of love.

John 3:16, *for God so loved the world that he gave His only begotten Son that whoever believes in Him shall not perish but have eternal life.*

Verses 10–11, *10 In this is love, not that we loved God, but that he loved us, and sent his Son as the atoning sacrifice for our sins. 11 Beloved, if God loved us in this way, we also ought to love one another.*

Reflection

As already mentioned, Greek for propitiation is *hilasterion*, which means mercy seat. The mercy seat was the golden cover on the ark of the covenant. In the Old Testament, the high priest entered the Holy of Holies to sprinkle the blood of the lamb upon the mercy seat as an atonement of sins for the Israelites for one year.

The NIV translates propitiation as atoning sacrifice. The mercy seat foreshadowed Christ's death on the cross as the atoning sacrifice for our sins. We are to love one another to reciprocate His love for us.

Application

Develop your discernment abilities by reflecting on them. Compare all spiritual teachings to Scripture and carefully examine any spirits that you encounter. This will help protect you from false doctrines and strengthen your faith in the gospel message.

Reconnect with the Holy Spirit by reflecting on your relationship. Seek guidance from Him and remember that the power of Christ inside is greater than Satan. This gives you the confidence to rely on Him in every situation and stand firm on your faith.

Love is a powerful emotion. Demonstrate your love for God by serving others in a selfless and genuine manner. Building deeper relationships with others and revealing more about God's character can be achieved by expressing and being open to His love.

Take a moment to consider the love of God. Jesus' sacrifice of selflessness is a sign of the overwhelming love from above. It encourages you to live a grateful life and show grace and kindness to others.

God is love. God demonstrated His amazing love for you by sending Jesus to the cross as an atoning sacrifice for your sins. You are justified by grace through faith in Christ.

God considered you just as if you had not sinned if you believe in His Son. Now that you are justified by grace, you have peace with God and you can come before Him in prayer with boldness and confidence.

Prayer

Heavenly Father, thank You for loving us even though we do not deserve it. Thank You for Your mercy and grace. We acknowledge that we were sinners and are saved by Your grace. Thank You for all that You have done for us in our lives. In Jesus' name, amen.

7

The Perfection of Love

Prayer

Heavenly Father, Jesus is Wonderful, the Counsellor, Prince of Peace, Mighty God, Everlasting Father, trinitarian God of the Bible, and the only true God. We pray for Your presence, anointing, revelation, and guidance. We pray for divine wisdom in understanding and applying Scripture. In Jesus' name, Amen.

1 John 4:12–21

Verses 12–13, *12 No one has seen God at any time. If we love one another, God remains in us, and his love has been perfected in us. 13 By this we know that we remain in him and he in us, because he has given us of his Spirit.*

Reflection

No one has ever seen God because He is invisible, but God manifested Himself to us by becoming fully human and fully divine in Christ. God's love will be made perfect in us if we love one another. Christ's love abiding in us through the Holy Spirit will enable us to love one another.

Colossians 1:15, *The Son is the image of the invisible God, the firstborn over all creation.*

John 1:14, *And the Word became flesh and dwelt among us, and we beheld His glory, the glory as of the only begotten of the Father, full of grace and truth.*

Verses 14–16, *14 We have seen and testify that the Father has sent the Son as the Savior of the world. 15 Whoever confesses that Jesus is the Son of God, God remains in him, and he in God. 16 We know and have believed the love which God has for us. God is love, and he who remains in love remains in God, and God remains in him.*

Reflection

John and the apostles saw and testified that God had sent Jesus into the world as Savior of the world. The test of a Christian is confessing Jesus as Son of God. Whoever confesses Jesus as Son of God abides in God and God abides in him. The test of a Christian is knowing and believing that God is love. Those who remain in love remain in God, and God remains in them.

Verses 17–19, *17 In this, love has been made perfect among us, that we may have boldness in the day of judgment, because as he is, even so we are in this world. 18 There is no fear in love; but perfect love casts out fear, because fear has punishment. He who fears is not made perfect in love. 19 We love him, because he first loved us.*

Reflection

Love is made perfect in us by the God of love. Love is the opposite of fear. Love speaks of rewards, but fear speaks of punishments. Those who love God will not fear His judgment. Those who love God can approach Him with confidence. We love God because He loved us first, 1 John 4:19.

Verses 20–21, *20 If a man says, "I love God," and hates his brother, he is a liar; for he who doesn't love his brother whom he has seen, how can he love God whom he has not seen? 21 This commandment we have from him, that he who loves God should also love his brother.*

Reflection

The test of a Christian is love. Failure to love our brother and sister proves that we do not love God. As already mentioned, we are to love God vertically and our brothers and sisters horizontally.

Application

Consider how God's love in your life is revealed through the way you treat others. Your actions are a demonstration of His love and character. You can show Him by demonstrating His love through your actions. By loving others, you will make His presence and love known.

Reevaluate your relationship to the Holy Spirit. Testify to Jesus's Savior and rely on His guidance. You can strengthen this bond by asking for His guidance in all areas of your life.

Let His love and unconditional affection guide your faith and your actions.

The three tests of a Christian are confessing Christ as Son of God, believing in God, and loving God. God is a God of love. John was the apostle of love.

As mentioned before, Greek for love in 1 John is *agape*, the highest form of love. Perfect love casts out fear of God's judgment.

Love is the greatest commandment and the greatest virtue. Therefore, you must love God and others just as Christ loves you.

Prayer

Heavenly Father, we are forever grateful to You for loving us and for sending Jesus as the atoning sacrifice for our sins. We pray for grace and divine enablement to love You vertically and one another horizontally. In Jesus' name, amen.

8

The Test for Loving God

Prayer

Heavenly Father, we acknowledge that You are Yahweh Rapha, Rohi, Jireh, Nissi, Tsidkenu, Shamma, Sabaoth, and Shalom. Thank You that You are all these and much more. There are no words to describe all of Your attributes and characteristics. We pray for Your Spirit of wisdom, understanding, knowledge, and obedience to reside in us. In Jesus' name, amen.

1 John 5:1–21

Verses 1–2, *1 Whoever believes that Jesus is the Christ has been born of God. Whoever loves the Father also loves the child who is born of him. 2 By this we know that we love the children of God, when we love God and keep his commandments.*

Reflection

The tests for loving God and of spiritual regeneration are to believe that Jesus is the Christ and to keep His commandments.

Verses 3–5, *3 For this is loving God, that we keep his commandments. His commandments are not grievous. 4 For whatever is born of God overcomes the world. This is the victory that has overcome the world: your faith. 5 Who is he who overcomes the world, but he who believes that Jesus is the Son of God?*

Reflection

We show our love for God by keeping His commandments. His commandments are not difficult to keep if we love Him. Spiritually regenerated people overcome the world by believing that Jesus is the Son of God.

Verses 6–8, *6 This is he who came by water and blood, Jesus Christ; not with the water only, but with the water and the blood. It is the Spirit who testifies, because the Spirit is the truth. 7 For there are three who testify: 8 the Spirit, the water, and the blood; and the three agree as one.*

Reflection

Jesus' incarnation through natural birth, by water and blood, was witnessed by the Holy Spirit, the Spirit of truth. There are three witnesses of Christ's incarnation in heaven: Father God, Jesus, the Word, and the Holy Spirit. There are three witnesses on earth: the Holy Spirit, the water, and the blood. Water may be a reference to Christ's birth or His baptism, and blood to His crucifixion.

Verses 9–10, *9 If we receive the witness of men, the witness of God is greater; for this is God's testimony which he has testified concerning his Son. 10 He who believes in the Son of God has the testimony in himself. He who doesn't believe God has made him a liar, because he has not believed in the testimony that God has given concerning his Son.*

Reflection

God's witness is greater than man's. God's witness testified to the authenticity of Jesus Christ. Those who believe in Jesus Christ believe in God's witness. Those who do not believe in Jesus Christ do not believe in God's witness.

Verses 11–12, *11 The testimony is this, that God gave to us eternal life, and this life is in his Son. 12 He who has the Son has the life. He who doesn't have God's Son doesn't have the life.*

Reflection

God gave us eternal life in Christ. Whoever has Christ has life; whoever does not have Christ does not have life. 1 John 5:12 is a promise to claim and a memory verse to memorize: *He who has the Son has the life. He who doesn't have God's Son doesn't have the life.*

Verse 13, *13 These things I have written to you who believe in the name of the Son of God, that you may know that you have eternal life, and that you may continue to believe in the name of the Son of God.*

Reflection

John reassured his audience, and us, to believe and continue believing in the name of Christ so that we will have eternal life.

Verses 14–15, *14 This is the boldness which we have toward him, that if we ask anything according to his will, he listens to us. 15 And if we know that he listens to us, whatever we ask, we know that we have the petitions which we have asked of him.*

Reflection

If we ask Christ anything according to His will, He will hear us. Since we know that He hears us, we have a basis to ask with boldness.

Verses 16-19, *16 If anyone sees his brother sinning a sin not leading to death, he shall ask, and God will give him life for those who sin not leading to death. There is a sin leading to death. I don't say that he should make a request concerning this. 17 All unrighteousness is sin, and there is a sin not leading to death. 18 We know that whoever is born of God doesn't sin, but he who was born of God keeps himself, and the evil one doesn't touch him. 19 We know that we are of God, and the whole world lies in the power of the evil one.*

Reflection

John encouraged his audience, and us, to pray for our brother who commits a pardonable sin. However, if someone blasphemes the Holy Spirit, this is unpardonable, and should not be prayed for.

Mark 3:28–29, *Assuredly, I say to you, all sins will be forgiven the sons of men, and whatever blasphemies they may utter, but he who blasphemes against the Holy Spirit never has forgiveness, but is subject to eternal condemnation.*

Reflection

John reminds his audience, and us, that spiritually regenerated Christians should not sin habitually because they belong to God.

Verses 20–21, *20 We know that the Son of God has come, and has given us an understanding, that we know him who is true, and we are in him who is true, in his Son Jesus Christ. This is the true God and eternal life. 21 Little children, keep yourselves from idols.*

Reflection

We belong to Jesus Christ, the only true God and source of eternal life. John warned his audience, and us, to keep away from idolatry.

Application

Rethink your faith in Jesus. Reaffirm daily that Jesus is the Christ, Son of God. Your faith will help you overcome life's obstacles with courage. This will help you live more boldly as a child of God.

Consider your obedience to God's commandments. Enjoy obeying God's commandments. They are not meant to burden you, but rather for your benefit. See obedience as a form of worship.

Be sure to carefully consider the testimony of God. Trust that God's Word and believe that Jesus is the only way to eternal life. This will help you to strengthen your faith.

Reflect on your own prayer life. As you pray, align your requests to God's will and approach Him with the confidence that He will hear and answer your prayers. This will increase your dependence on Him and deepen your relationship with Him.

Think about how you intercede for others. Pray for other believers who are struggling with sin. Pray for people who are engaging in harmful behaviors by asking God to restore life and restore them. This practice creates a caring and supportive atmosphere within the Christian community.

Reevaluate the way you fight sin. Turn to Jesus for help to avoid evil. To be free of persistent sin, you must examine yourself and seek God's help to remove it from your life.

Explore your understanding of God. Through study, reflection, and prayer, I will increase my knowledge of Him, His truth, and the truths that He teaches. I trust Jesus to lead me down this path. This will enrich your spiritual life and deepen your relationship to God.

Remove idols that could threaten to replace God as your Lord. Be aware of any signs of idolatry and make sure that nothing in your life is more important than Him. Keep an eye out for signs to ensure that you devote yourself and worship only Him.

The tests of loving God and of spiritual regeneration are faith and obedience. Believe that Jesus is the Christ, the Son of God who came to earth through His incarnation to save sinners.

Prayer

Heavenly Father, we pray that You will give us the grace to love You and one another. We pray that You will keep us away from idolatry and keep us in the faith. Thank You for the gift of eternal life and the promise of heaven. In Jesus' name, amen.

9

2 John: Walk in Truth and Obedience

Introduction

Scholars agree that the epistle of 2 John was written by the apostle John, who wrote 1 John around the same time, AD 85–95. John wrote this epistle to warn his audience against the same Gnostic teachers.

Prayer

Heavenly Father, we pray that You will enlighten our spiritual insight and help us to study your Word with confidence. We pray that we will abide in You and Your words will abide in us. In Jesus' name, amen.

2 John 1–13

Verses 1–3, *1 The elder, to the chosen lady and her children, whom I love in truth, and not I only, but also all those who know the truth, 2 for the truth's sake, which remains in us, and it will be with us forever: 3 Grace, mercy, and peace will be with us, from God the Father, and from the Lord Jesus Christ, the Son of the Father, in truth and love.*

Reflection

John, the Elder, wrote this epistle to the elect lady and her children. Scholars are not in agreement as to the identity of this elect lady, whether this was a real person or a figure of speech for a church. Her children refer to the Christians in the region of Ephesus. John loved them in truth and prayed that truth would abide in them forever. He pronounced grace, mercy, and peace on them from God the Father and Jesus the Son, in truth and love.

Verses 4–6, *4 I rejoice greatly that I have found some of your children walking in truth, even as we have been commanded by the Father. 5 Now I beg you, dear lady, not as though I wrote to you a new commandment, but that which we had from the beginning, that we love one another. 6 This is love, that we should walk according to his commandments. This is the commandment, even as you heard from the beginning, that you should walk in it.*

Reflection

John rejoiced that his audience was walking in truth, obedience, and love. The test of loving Christ is obedience to his commandment to love.

Verses 7–11, *7 For many deceivers have gone out into the world, those who don't confess that Jesus Christ came in the flesh. This is the deceiver and the Antichrist. 8 Watch yourselves, that we don't lose the things which we have accomplished, but that we receive a full reward. 9 Whoever transgresses and doesn't remain in the teaching of Christ, doesn't have God. He who remains in the teaching has both the Father and the Son. 10 If anyone comes to you, and doesn't bring this teaching, don't receive him into your house, and don't welcome him, 11 for he who welcomes him participates in his evil deeds.*

Reflections

"Deceivers" speaks of the heretical Gnostic teachers, who rejected the incarnation of Christ and had the spirit of antichrist. Those who follow the false doctrines of the Gnostics do not know God. John warned his audience to reject these teachers, not to invite them into their houses, and not even to greet them.

Verses 12–13, *12 Having many things to write to you, I don't want to do so with paper and ink, but I hope to come to you, and to speak face to face, that our joy may be made full. 13 The children of your chosen sister greet you. Amen.*

Reflections

John hoped to be able to meet his audience personally to share in their joy. He sent them greetings from their elect sister—possibly a member of the local church where he was a member.

Application

Live out your commitment to love and truth in your everyday life. When acting or talking, aim for honesty and sincerity. This will reflect

God's character by your actions or words. It is important to be honest, sincere, and kind in your actions or words on God's behalf.

Consider obedience an act of devotion, since obedience shows you reverence and devotion to Him. As part of your demonstration of love for Him, incorporate biblical principles into all of your decisions and interactions.

Consider your understanding of spiritual deception. Keep an eye out for falsehoods and be vigilant when discerning the truth. By studying Scripture and consulting trusted spiritual leaders, you can ensure that any teaching or belief aligns with Jesus Christ's truth.

Reexamine your commitment to Christ's teaching. Prioritize learning and adhering to His words. This will help you develop your relationship with Him as well as community participation. Reading the Bible regularly, praying and participating are all essential.

Be aware of your associations and relationships. Reject any false teachings. Use judicious judgment in your relationships, and do not encourage those who spread misinformation.

Prioritize meaningful face-to-face interaction with family members and other believers. These encounters will create joy and deeper understanding.

Do not be deceived by false preachers who claim to be from God but are not. Today, many false teachers are preaching heretical doctrines and peddling false theology.

These people are dangerous and are like wolves in sheepskins. The only sure way to discern false doctrine is by having a strong foundation in the Word of God.

2 Timothy 2:15, *Do your best to present yourself to God as one approved, a worker who does not need to be ashamed and who correctly handles the word of truth.*

Prayer

Heavenly Father, we pray for wisdom and discernment to test every spirit because not all spirits are from You. We pray for the spirit of wisdom, understanding, discernment, and insight to rightly divide the Word of truth, to discern and reject false doctrines. In Jesus' name, amen.

10

3 John: Reject Evil, Imitate Good

Introduction

Scholars agree that the author of 3 John is John the apostle, who wrote this general epistle around the same time as 1 and 2 John, between AD 85 and 95. John rebuked Diotrephes, a dictatorial leader in the church around Ephesus who rejected itinerant teachers sent by John and had excommunicated those who supported these teachers. The epistle was written to Gaius, who supported John's itinerant teachers.

Prayer

Heavenly Father, we pray that You will open our spiritual eyes, ears, and hearts to understand Scripture and wisdom, and to apply spiritual truth to our lives. We pray that You will speak to each of us individually through Your Word. In Jesus' name, amen.

3 John 1–14, Gaius, Diotrephes, and Demetrius

Verses 1–4, *1 The elder to Gaius the beloved, whom I love in truth. 2 Beloved, I pray that you may prosper in all things and be healthy, even as your soul prospers. 3 For I rejoiced greatly when brothers came and testified about your truth, even as you walk in truth. 4 I have no greater joy than this: to hear about my children walking in truth.*

Reflection

This epistle from John, the Elder, was addressed to the beloved Gaius, whom he loved in truth. John prayed for Gaius' health, an material and spiritual prosperity. He rejoiced when other Christians testified to him that Gaius was walking in the truth.

Verses 5–8, *5 Beloved, you do a faithful work in whatever you accomplish for those who are brothers and strangers. 6 They have testified about your love before the assembly. You will do well to send them forward on their journey in a way worthy of God, 7 because for the sake of the Name they went out, taking nothing from the Gentiles. 8 We therefore ought to receive such, that we may be fellow workers for the truth.*

Reflection

John commended Gaius for his generosity in showing hospitality and looking after the needs of itinerant teachers sent to him.

Verses 9–10, *9 I wrote to the assembly, but Diotrephes, who loves to be first among them, doesn't accept what we say. 10 Therefore if I come, I will call attention to his deeds which he does, unjustly accusing us with wicked words. Not content with this, neither does he himself receive the brothers, and those who would, he forbids and throws out of the assembly.*

Reflection

John rebuked a dictatorial leader called Diotrephes, who rejected teachers John had sent to the churches in the region of Ephesus. Diotrephes had even excommunicated those who supported the itinerant preachers.

Verses 11–12, *11 Beloved, don't imitate that which is evil, but that which is good. He who does good is of God. He who does evil hasn't seen God.*

Reflection

John warned his audience, and us, not to do evil but to do good. Those who do good are from God, but those who do evil do not know God. John commended Demetrius, who had a good testimony.

Verses 13–14, *13 I had many things to write to you, but I am unwilling to write to you with ink and pen; 14 but I hope to see you soon. Then we will speak face to face. Peace be to you. The friends greet you. Greet the friends by name.*

Reflection

John wanted to write a longer letter but preferred to speak to them in person when visiting them soon. He pronounced peace on them as a farewell greeting.

Application

Reconsider your commitments to truth and faithfulness. Follow Gaius by living by your convictions and showing love to others.

Consider how you show hospitality to others in ministry and provide support. Support fellow believers and show kindness to strangers who are serving God's Kingdom.

Reexamine your response to leadership and influence. Avoid selfish ambitions and make sure your actions reflect God's standards of kindness, hospitality, and generosity. This may include being selective in who you choose to associate with and actively advocating what's just and honorable.

Consider your attitude toward fellow believers. Encourage and reward those who are faithful in serving God. This will strengthen unity and morale in Christian communities.

Think about how you interact with the members of your church. Prioritize face-to-face interaction between believers to foster personal connections and mutual encouragement. This approach will deepen spiritual ties while fostering unity.

Do good and not evil. Do not to imitate Diotrephes, the dictatorial leader, but imitate Gaius and Demetrius who supported preachers and teachers of the Word. There is no place for dictatorial leaders in the Kingdom of God.

Prayer

Heavenly Father, thank You for speaking to us through the epistles of 1, 2, and 3 John. Thank You for their messages that transcend time, culture, geography, history, and language. Help us to have a strong foundation in the Word so as not to be deceived by false doctrines. In Jesus' name, amen.

11

Jude: Now unto Him Who Is Able to Keep You from Falling

Prayer

Heavenly Father, we acknowledge that Jesus Christ is the Bread of Life, the Light of the world, the Gate, the Good Shepherd, the Resurrection and the Life, the Way, the Truth, and the Life, and the True Vine, teach us Your Word. We pray that You will help us to unlock the book of Jude and give us the keys to understanding and application. In Jesus' name, amen.

Introduction

Scholars agree that the author of Jude is Jude, the half-brother of Jesus Christ and brother of James the just. The letter is believed to have been written around AD 65. This is a general epistle written to all Jewish and Gentile Christians to warn them against the immoral, false, ungodly, Gnostic teachers who maintained that salvation by grace is a license to sin.

Matthew 13:55, *is this not the carpenter's son? Is not His mother called Mary? And His brothers James, Joses, Simon, and Judas?*

Mark 6:3, *"is this not the carpenter, the Son of Mary, and brother of James, Joses, Judas, and Simon? And are not His sisters here with us?" So they were offended at Him.*

Verses 1–2, *1 Jude, a servant of Jesus Christ, and brother of James, to those who are called, sanctified by God the Father, and kept for Jesus Christ: 2 May mercy, peace, and love be multiplied to you.*

Reflection

Jude identified himself as a bondservant or slave of Jesus Christ, and a brother of James. His audience was those sanctified by God and preserved by Jesus Christ. Greek for "preserved" is *tereo*, which means kept. Greek for "called" is *kletos*, which means called. Christians are divinely called by God and kept in the faith by Jesus Christ. Jude pronounced mercy, peace, and love to his audience.

Verses 3–4, *3 Beloved, while I was very eager to write to you about our common salvation, I was constrained to write to you exhorting you to contend earnestly for the faith which was once for all delivered to the saints. 4 For there are certain men who crept in secretly, even those who were long ago written about for this condemnation: ungodly men, turning the grace of our God into indecency, and denying our only Master, God, and Lord, Jesus Christ.*

Reflection

Jude initially wanted to write a general letter on salvation but changed his mind when he saw immoral and ungodly men who perverted the grace of God and taught wrong doctrines to the Christians.

Verse 5, *5 Now I desire to remind you, though you already know this, that the Lord, having saved a people out of the land of Egypt, afterward destroyed those who didn't believe.*

Reflection

God delivered the Jews under the leadership of Moses out of Egypt but, because of unbelief, they perished in the wilderness. Only Joshua and Caleb made it into the Promised Land after 40 years of wilderness wandering.

Verse 6, *6 Angels who didn't keep their first domain, but deserted their own dwelling place, he has kept in everlasting bonds under darkness for the judgment of the great day.*

Reflection

This verse supports the view that in Genesis 6:4 fallen angels had sex with women on earth and produced giants. These fallen angels were to be kept locked up in a place called Tartarus.

Genesis 6:4, *There were giants on the earth in those days, and also afterward when the sons of God came in to the daughters of men and they bore children to them. Those were the mighty men who were of old, men of renown.*

Verses 7-8, *7 Even as Sodom and Gomorrah and the cities around them, having in the same way as these given themselves over to sexual immorality and gone after strange flesh, are shown as an example, suffering the punishment of eternal fire. 8 Yet in the same way, these also in their dreaming defile the flesh, despise authority, and slander celestial beings.*

Reflection

The Gnostic teachers behaved like the people of Sodom and Gomorrah of Genesis 19. God destroyed Sodom and Gomorrah because of immorality and sexual perversion.

Genesis 19:29, *So when God destroyed the cities of the plain, he remembered Abraham, and he brought Lot out of the catastrophe that overthrew the cities where Lot had lived.*

Verse 9, *9 But Michael, the archangel, when contending with the devil and arguing about the body of Moses, dared not bring against him an abusive condemnation, but said, "May the Lord rebuke you!"*

Reflection

God buried Moses after his death and his body was never found. According to Jude, Satan disputed with God over Moses' body. But the archangel Michael challenged Satan, saying, *The Lord rebuke you!*

Verse 10, *10 But these speak evil of whatever things they don't know. They are destroyed in these things that they understand naturally, like the creatures without reason.*

The Gnostic teachers spoke evil, behaved like beasts, and were corrupt in their activities.

Verse 11, *11 Woe to them! For they went in the way of Cain, and ran riotously in the error of Balaam for hire, and perished in Korah's rebellion.*

Reflection

These immoral, heretical, Gnostic teachers behaved like Cain, Balaam, and Korah of the Old Testament.

The story of Cain is found in Genesis 4. Cain and Abel were brothers. God accepted Abel's offering but rejected Cain's because Abel offered a better sacrifice than Cain. Out of jealousy and wickedness, Cain murdered his brother.

The story of Balaam is found in Numbers 22–24. Balaam was a greedy false prophet who accepted a bribe from the Moabite king Balak to curse Israel. Every time Balaam wanted to curse Israel, he ended up blessing Israel.

The story of Korah is found in Numbers 16. Korah and his followers were Levites who challenged the leadership of Moses and Aaron. God opened the ground under their feet and buried them and their families alive.

Verses 12–13, *12 These are hidden rocky reefs in your love feasts when they feast with you, shepherds who without fear feed themselves; clouds without water, carried along by winds; autumn trees without fruit, twice dead, plucked up by the roots; 13 wild waves of the sea, foaming out their own shame; wandering stars, for whom the blackness of darkness has been reserved forever*

Reflection

The Lord's Supper in the first-century church was also called the love or agape feast. These false teachers would come to the love feasts and serve themselves, behave badly, cause harm, and deceive the Christians.

Acts 2:46–47, *Every day they continued to meet together in the temple courts. They broke bread in their homes and ate together with glad and sincere hearts, 47 praising God and enjoying the favor of all the people. And the Lord added to their number daily those who were being saved.*

1 Corinthians 11:20–21, *So then, when you come together, it is not the Lord's Supper you eat, for when you are eating, some of you go ahead with your own private suppers. As a result, one person remains hungry and another gets drunk.*

Verses 14–15, *14 About these also Enoch, the seventh from Adam, prophesied, saying, Behold, the Lord came with ten thousands of his holy ones, 15 to execute judgment on all, and to convict all the ungodly of all their works of ungodliness which they have done in an ungodly way, and of all the hard things which ungodly sinners have spoken against him.*

Reflection

Enoch was the seventh descendant of Adam from the line of Seth. Verses 14b–15 are a quotation from the book of *Enoch*, a pseudo-epigraphical book, which is not part of the Christian canon.

Verses 16–19, *16 These are murmurers and complainers, walking after their lusts—and their mouth speaks proud things—showing respect of persons to gain advantage. 17 But you, beloved, remember the words which have been spoken before by the apostles of our Lord Jesus Christ. 18 They said to you, "In the last time there will be mockers, walking after their own ungodly lusts." 19 These are those who cause divisions and are sensual, not having the Spirit.*

Reflection

The false teachers grumbled and complained and were boastful, lustful, ungodly, opportunistic, and dishonest. Jude reminded his audience to remember and hold fast to the words of the apostles.

Verses 20–23, *20 But you, beloved, keep building up yourselves on your most holy faith, praying in the Holy Spirit. 21 Keep yourselves in God's love, looking for the mercy of our Lord Jesus Christ to eternal life. 22 On some have compassion, making a distinction, 23 and some save, snatching them out of the fire with fear, hating even the clothing stained by the flesh.*

Reflection

Jude encouraged his audience to live holy lives, to pray in the Holy Spirit, and to love God. He encouraged his audience to have compassion on some and to save others by pulling them out from sin and judgment.

Verses 24–25, *24 Now to him who is able to keep them from stumbling, and to present you faultless before the presence of his glory in great joy, 25 to God our Savior, who alone is wise, be glory and majesty, dominion and power, both now and forever. Amen.*

Reflection

The epistle of Jude ends with a beautiful doxology, giving praise, honor, and glory to God, our Savior.

Application

Reflect on your commitment to the true faith. Actively combat false teachings, and make it clear that you will not tolerate them. Study the Bible with care and discernment to identify any harmful doctrines.

Think about your attitude towards sin and ungodliness. Cultivate a fear of God's judgement, remembering His justice, and righteousness. This will motivate you to live a holy life and pursue righteousness in your life.

Reflect on the spiritual growth you have experienced and your prayer life. Extend your faith and pray with the Holy Spirit. To deepen your relationship with God, commit to spiritual practices like studying the Bible, and praying regularly with other believers.

Consider your compassion for others and how you can help spread the gospel. Find ways to be kind to people who are struggling with their faith or have doubts. Spread the message of salvation and emphasize the importance of saving souls.

As you embark on your spiritual journey, remind yourself to trust God's faithfulness. You can overcome any fear and uncertainty by submitting them to God in faith. He will protect and lead you. This can bring hope and help strengthen your resolve to live faithfully to His glory

The epistle of Jude reminds us that there are false teachers out there who come as wolves in sheepskins to deceive Christians. Be vigilant, counter check with Scripture, and build a strong foundation through diligent Bible study.

Acts 17:11, *These were more noble than those in Thessalonica, in that they received the word with all readiness of mind, and searched the scriptures daily, whether those things were so.*

Prayer

Heavenly Father, thank You for speaking to us through the epistles of 1, 2, and 3 John, and Jude. Thank You for preserving Your inspired, inerrant, and infallible Word for thousands of years for our benefit. Thank You for Your amazing love. In Jesus' name, amen.

One Last Thing

Thank you for choosing to read my book. I hope that it has provided you with an enjoyable and thought-provoking experience. I would love to hear your feedback on the book, and I would be incredibly grateful if you could take the time to write a review on the platform where you purchased it or on a book review website. Your review will not only help other potential readers in making their decision but also help me to understand what worked and what didn't work in the book. Your honest review will help me improve as a writer and create even better content in the future. Once again, thank you for giving my book a chance, and I sincerely hope that you found it worth your time.

Dr. Andrew C. S. Koh

Scan the QR code for a free e-book

Scan the QR Code

Don't miss out!

Visit the website below and you can sign up to receive emails whenever Dr Andrew C S Koh publishes a new book. There's no charge and no obligation.

https://books2read.com/r/B-A-FMXV-QIEDC

BOOKS 2 READ

Connecting independent readers to independent writers.

Did you love *1 John, 2 John, 3 John & Jude: a Verse by Verse Bible Study*?
Then you should read *General Epistles: 1 Peter, 2 Peter, James*[1] by Dr
Andrew C S Koh!

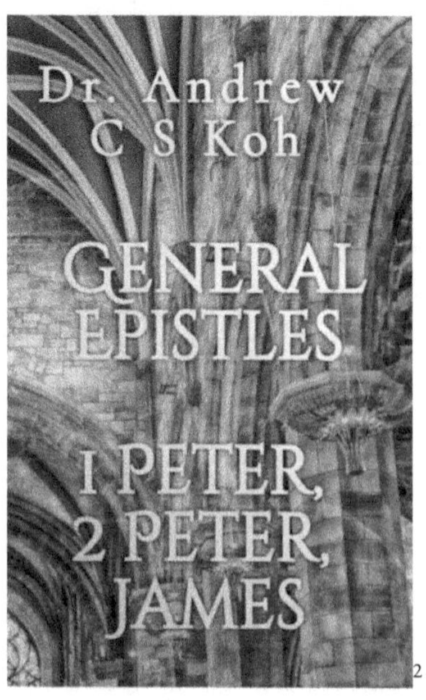

Dr. Andrew C.S. Koh's book, General Epistles, is a must-read for
Christians of all maturity levels. This 3-in-1 guide of 1 Peter, 2 Peter,
and James provides a comprehensive Bible study and devotional guide to
help readers grow in the knowledge of the grace of our Lord and Savior,
Jesus Christ. The book is divided into 16 lessons, each containing a
prayer, reflection, application, and prayer. By reflecting on the teachings
of scripture and applying them to our lives, we can learn to properly
understand and interpret the word of truth. 2 Timothy 3:16–17 states,
"All scripture is given by inspiration of God and is profitable for doctrine,

---

1. https://books2read.com/u/mqXJZZ

2. https://books2read.com/u/mqXJZZ

for reproof, for correction, for instruction in righteousness, that the man of God may be complete and thoroughly equipped for every good work."

1 Peter and 2 Peter contain important teachings to counter false prophets, apostates, and heresies that are widespread in modern churches. Dr. Koh's book provides a clear background and simple explanations of every passage. It is an invaluable tool for those seeking to grow spiritually and mature in their faith. Perfect for anyone looking to gain a deeper understanding of the Bible, General Epistles by Dr. Andrew C.S. Koh will take readers into the depths of the Word of God. Read this book to gain a clearer understanding of the scriptures and be equipped to stand firm against false teachings.

Read more at https://www.drandrewcskoh.com.

Also by Dr Andrew C S Koh

Daily Devotion
Manna of Life: Daily Devotion

Daily Devotions
Bread of Life Daily Devotions
Words of Eternal Life
Bread From Heaven: Daily Devotions
Light of the World Daily Devotions
Light of the World Daily Devotions
The Way, the Truth, and the Life

Genesis
Understanding Genesis 1-11: From Adam to Abraham
Faith Journey of Abraham: Genesis 12-25
Life Story of Jacob: Genesis 26-36
The Story of Joseph: Genesis 37-50

Gospels and Act

The Gospel According to Matthew
Daily Devotion Gospel of Mark
The Gospel According to Luke
Daily Devotion Gospel of John
Acts: Volume 1 and 2, From Jerusalem to Rome

Non Pauline and General Epistles
Hebrews: the Just Shall Live by Faith
1 John, 2 John, 3 John & Jude: a Verse by Verse Bible Study
General Epistles: 1 Peter, 2 Peter, James

Pauline Epistles
Romans: The Just Shall Live by Faith
1 Corinthians: The Greatest of These is Love
2 Corinthians: My Grace is Sufficient for You
1 Thessalonians, 2 Thessalonians, Philemon
Pastoral Epistles: 1 Timothy, 2 Timothy, Titus
Galatians: Justified by Faith in Jesus Christ
Philemon: Charge to the Master's Account

Prison Epistles
The Prison Epistles
Philippians: Rejoice Always in the Lord
Colossians: He is the Image of the Invisible God
Ephesians: Every Spiritual Blessing in the Heavenly Places in Christ

Standalone
Apocalypse: Understanding the Book of Revelation
Expository Preaching
Memoirs of a Doctor
Moses: Let My People Go
The ABCS of Self-Publishing
Living Word Living Savior: a Portrait of Jesus Through the Eyes of John

Watch for more at https://www.drandrewcskoh.com.

About the Author

Dr. Andrew C. S. Koh is a Christian author who has published 36 books. Beyond his role as an author, he is also a blogger, podcaster, bible teacher, digital creator, and retired cardiologist. He pursued theology at Laidlaw College in Auckland, New Zealand in 1999. Currently residing in Malaysia with his family, he finds joy in coffee, travel, and photography. He is listed in the Malaysia Book of Records for having the Most Books Published and Released in 2021.

Find out more about Andrew on:

https://linktr.ee/andrewcskoh

Search Andrew's books on:

https://books2read.com/ap/xX066D/Dr-Andrew-C-S-Koh

Get your free books on:

https://storyoriginapp.com/giveaways/b295be58-7736-11ec-ac4b-e34d930c508e

https://books2read.com/u/3kYJlN

Read more at https://www.drandrewcskoh.com.

About the Publisher

Dr. Andrew C. S. Koh, a bestselling Amazon author, has authored 36 Christian books covering the New Testament, Old Testament, Bible study guides, and devotionals. Beyond his role as an author, he is a blogger, podcaster, bible teacher, and cardiologist. He pursued theology at Laidlaw College in Auckland, New Zealand in 1999.. Currently residing in Malaysia with his family, he finds joy in coffee, travel, and photography. He is listed in the Malaysia Book of Records for having the Most Books Published and Released in 2021.

Author of Memoirs of a Doctor:

https://dl.bookfunnel.com/hm2npovxom

Link Tree:

https://linktr.ee/andrewcskoh

Universal book link:

https://books2read.com/ap/xX066D/Dr-Andrew-C-S-Koh

New Release Notification:

https://books2read.com/author/dr-andrew-c-s-koh/subscribe/1/384961/

Free Books:

https://storyoriginapp.com/giveaways/b295be58-7736-11ec-ac4b-e34d930c508e

https://books2read.com/u/3kYJlN

Read more at https://www.drandrewcskoh.com.